Our
Broken
Compass

CALVIN
RICHARDSON

outskirts
press

Acknowledgements

First, I would like to thank my wife who is also my editor, proof reader, and encourager. Delois Ann has been my stabilizer for over fifty years. She is God's special blessing to me. My Children and grandchildren are my continuing inspiration. They truly are the reason I write at all. Three teachers encouraged me through the years. My fourth grade teacher, Mr. Carlson, assured me that I would become a great writer, and Mrs. Monahan, my eighth grade teacher insisted that I had a future in poetry. My college professor, J. Paul, encouraged me to keep writing and improving what skills I had. God bless them all. I also want to thank Deni Sinteral-Scott at Outskirts Press for her graciousness, patience and general assistance in getting my books published. Thanks to each and every one who has contributed to the books I've written. I hope I have done them justice.

On a ship there is a hierarchy, a chain of command through which information required to accomplish the mission of the vessel is channeled. The bridge is where leadership sets the course and manages the function of the ship. The compass is the basic guide for setting the course of the ship. Initial guidance comes from the bridge and is filtered down through various division chiefs and department heads. In these divisions or departments are the people who implement instructions and put orders into action. These actions make the vessel an instrument that is able to meet requirements of the assigned mission.

The fantail is at the aft (rear) of the ship. On the fantail men and women who put the instructions from the bridge into action sometimes gather to exchange opinions on, or discuss the quality and effectiveness of the direction they receive. The fantail becomes especially vocal when guidance from the bridge fails to accomplish the task at hand and that guidance seems to defy common sense and logic.

Governments function in a similar manner. Guidance, in the form of rules, regulations and laws, comes from the highest elected authority to be disseminated by a descending order of bureaucracy. Citizens are subject to, and the ultimate implementers of, those rules and laws. They gather in various forums to discuss their perspective on the propriety or impropriety of those rules, regulations and laws. The citizens become more vocal as the guidance from "higher authority" appears to lack prudence and wisdom. As a former member of the group that gathered on the fantail; now retired, I share my opinion as a member of the citizens group. What I have written here is a result of years of discussion and observation from hearts and minds of the men and women who endeavor to make the vessel, or the nation, function as it was designed to.

This is an opinion that recognizes and laments the lack of intellect and common sense among our elected representatives, as they direct the functioning of our government, and within our citizenship as we select our leaders.

The Founding Fathers set the destination and provided the compass to keep the ship of state on course. We, the citizens, are tasked to maintain the nation and we are integral to the accomplishment of the mission assigned. We seem to be failing in our responsibility while excusing ourselves by blaming those we elect. Therefore, you might refer to this endeavor as "Leadership from the Bridge; Commentary from the Fantail". This commentary is an observation with opinion.

Leadership is a mandatory quality for success on all endeavors, whether governmental, business, military or family. Great leadership cannot succeed without committed and dynamic subordinates to support that leadership. However, great leadership can make poor progress if those they lead will not meet their responsibilities as followers.

Table of Contents

The Broken Compass

The problem, which has evolved since the adoption of our Constitution, seems to have begun almost immediately. Every generation since has an embedded assumption that their situation is worse than ever before. Some aspects may be better, but for the most part the situation is deteriorating. My generation is no different. We're pretty certain that the nation abandoned the Constitution, and common sense, in earnest since the decade of the fifties.

After WWII and the Korean Conflict, the United States entered a period of prosperity. While the economy began to thrive, the culture began to decline. The men and women who had endured the world's struggles through the 30's and 40's adopted the attitude that their children would have it better in every way than they had. They would be better housed, better clothed, better educated, better entertained and, the more ominous goal, more secure.

The wars had brought the nation into more intimate contact with other cultures and other political ideologies. It gradually became acceptable to embrace all cultures as equal and all forms of government as worthy of the utmost respect. They were equal without regard to their ideology or its consequences to their citizens and to the world at large. This "tolerance" is presently referred to as "political correctness" and the euphemistic goal of the universal tolerance is the illusive universal peace and cooperation. Political correctness is tolerant of any and all ideas and ideals except those that call them to task for the failure to use common sense and logic. Everything is wonderful except pointing out that it is really not wonderful at all. This ideology has been labeled with the benign sounding, forward looking, title "Progressive".

However, along with more tolerance and better security came less discipline, less responsibility. As the economy boomed, our cultural values declined. With the increase in wealth came an increase in rudeness, vulgarity, profanity, crudeness, and amoral behavior. It has also become more and more the general opinion that other cultures were more sophisticated, better educated, and more to be envied, than our own. In fact, a common allegation is that we, the citizens of the United States of America, have no culture of our own. Oh no... we are not a melting pot whose culture is the combination of the best parts of the numerous cultures that made America great, we are a "salad bowl" of a multitude of cultures that are separate; unique. There are no Americans...there are only hyphenated groups of citizens, loyal to their mother countries and their cultures. Italian-Americans, German-Americans, African Americans, Polish Americans; but no real Americans. Even the indigenous people are not Americans, they are tribes of people within the nation who are separated by their history and culture. All individuals, all equal, all perfectly in tune with their nature and their faith. Unlike those who profess to be Americans and give little credence to the salad bowl that purports to be filled with wonderful people. Persons totally unlike those bigoted Americans who live to persecute all other cultures and nationalities.

The Marshall Plan rebuilt the economies and the infrastructure of nations the Allies had defeated after World War II, and though we were certain we were the most powerful nation on earth, our self confidence did not extend to include our cultural values. As our culture embraced new levels of "tolerance", respect for our Constitution and its founders and our history declined. As the "Progressive" movement began to infiltrate our educational system the nation's self esteem began to be eroded.

Society, in general, adopted the premise that we should be more tolerant of the government enlarging its power to assure our personal security. We have become less devoted to the ideal that our Constitution should be held in highest esteem, and that big government be continually guarded against. The culture has abandoned the primary premise that implementation of the law must adhere to the pursuit of individual freedom and dignity. Tolerance of a federal government that interferes with personal responsibility, dilutes family values, abandons traditional values, and adopts a "tolerant" excuse for every immoral and amoral activity, permeates our culture. These excuses usually involve blaming anything and anyone for our problems except ourselves, the actual perpetrators. When a reasonably acceptable blame cannot be found and applied as an excuse, there are the bedrock villains—religious zealotry, racism, homophobia, xenophobia, as well as a plethora of other "phobias" to fall back on. When racism or religious intolerance are labeled as the culprit, government intervention is demanded. The change has been pervasive, invading, not only individual values, but also family values and the cultural values of our society and of our governing ideology. The desire to adopt a more open-minded, politically correct culture, has opened the door to unintended consequences that have led to the situation we find ourselves in today.

> *"They that can give up essential liberty to obtain a little temporary safety deserve neither liberty nor safety." —Benjamin Franklin*

It has resulted in a decline in our educational system, the destruction of the family unit, the invasion of our privacy by government, and the abandoning of the basic tenets on which the nation had been founded.

> *"Liberty cannot be preserved without a general knowledge among the people, who have a right, from the frame of their nature, to knowledge, as their great Creator, who does nothing in vain, has given them understandings, and a desire to know; but besides this, they have a right, an indisputable, unalienable, indefeasible, divine right to that most dreaded and envied kind of knowledge; I mean, of the characters and conduct of their rulers." —John Adams, Dissertation on Canon and Feudal Law, 1765*

The government was designed as a system of checks and balances. Gradually, as the nation matured the checks and balances have shifted significantly. Early on in the nation's history, the balance between the executive, judicial and legislative branches began to shift. President Jackson, who I admire for his courage and decisiveness, was also one of the most egregious violators of the system of checks and balances. When checked by the Supreme Court in his efforts to exert executive power to accomplish unconstitutional purposes, he is alleged to have said, "the Court has made their ruling and now let them enforce it". Then he proceeded to continue in his violation of the Constitution and moved the indigenous Americans from their homelands in the Eastern United States to west of the Mississippi.

Gradually the executive branch has usurped or been allowed powers that were never intended. Meanwhile the legislature has waxed and waned in its responsibilities and now is a relatively impotent branch of the government. The Judiciary has become an adjunct political arm of the party in power. Instead of retaining the apolitical position and adhering to clear and concise rulings that defer to the Constitution, the Court wavers along embellishing its decisions with current social and political trends and even at times including influence of foreign nations' legal decisions in making their rulings.

We emphasize that it is American conceptions of decency that are dispositive, rejecting the contention...that the...practices of other countries are relevant. — United States Supreme Court, Stanford v. Kentucky, 492 U.S. 361, 369 n.1 (1989)

The objective of the Supreme Court is to assure adherence to the Constitution. It is not and was not intended that the Court's duty is to assist the Executive and Legislative branches in finding ways to circumvent the Constitution.

The time has come for those of us who have been standing on the sidelines, for a couple of generations, to step up and be heard. We have assumed, naively, that our elected representatives would never let our freedom be eroded. After all, are they Americans too; freedom loving, patriotic, and proud of the nation's history and progress... or not? We are beginning to realize that federal and state administrations, with the misguided support of our representatives, and the lack of attention by the citizens, are encroaching on every aspect of our lives. They, the federal and state governing bodies, are regulating what we eat, how we care for and educate our children, how we manage our health care, what we drive, how we save our money, and spend our money, what kind of light bulbs we can buy, how we arrange for our retirement, and on and on.

Though we are loath to admit it, our nation has an elitist segment of society. They are the independently wealthy and the politicians. The elitists enjoy a degree of freedom that most of the population can't appreciate, exercising this freedom regardless of the governing ideology in power. Unfortunately, an accumulation of great wealth is often equated as an indicator of superior intellect and premier qualification for leadership. Evidence to the contrary is abundant but, because the majority of the population is poorly informed, those who are in authority find themselves routinely elected and re-elected to these positions. The result of this is that we have politicians who have no appreciation of the danger to freedom when government interference intrudes into our personal lives. The political elite are unfazed by the laws that usurp individual freedom and aggravate the majority of the population because they are insulated by their wealth and position.

Though their ignorant mandates rarely conform to the Constitution these mandates are becoming the law of the land. Traditional "right and wrong" are being replaced by values guided by "politically correctness" and "situational ethics". What is politically acceptable is dictated by government rules and regulations and enforced by bureaucrats. If you disagree with them you may well be subject to legal action instituted by the government, the same government that you have assumed is there to guarantee that your freedom is assured and protected. Laws have been instituted, and more are being proposed, that will endeavor to institute moral values that meet the demands of the culture of "political correctness".[1]

Do we really need laws to regulate every choice we are confronted with? Does the government have the right, and the responsibility, to dictate the correctness of every choice we make? There was a time when we had the freedom to make choices for ourselves with the understanding that each choice we made had consequences. We learned to differentiate between good choices and poor choices from experiencing the consequences of decisions we made. We learned there were winners and losers, we learned the rules; we knew what was right and what was wrong. Justice and injustice were part of our continuing education from the games we played to the books we read. We were free to choose, and poor choices had unpleasant consequences. Admittedly, the right choices were not always made, bad things happened; justice was not always accomplished, but what was just and right was understood to be the common goal of the society and the culture. We learned to recognize what worked and what didn't. Honesty, loyalty, integrity, and the golden rule were good, to cheat, lie, steal, and treat others cruelly was bad. Freedom, self-reliance, and respect for self and others were to be cherished as worthy to be aspired to. Unnecessary dependence on others, demanding that your needs and wants be provided without any effort from you, was frowned upon.

In the United States of America, the state was never intended to control our life from cradle to grave. The Founding Fathers instituted a form of government that limited the Federal government's ability to invade the private lives of citizens. Those "rich, old, white men", could read the works of the great philosophers in Latin, Greek, French and English, were accomplished in mathematics, sciences, and history. They also had a deep-seated understanding of, and respect for, individual freedom. Those men, who founded this United States over two hundred years ago and instituted a system that produced the most affluent and influential country in the world's history, knew what they were doing. Today they are ridiculed by professors and politicians, educators, students, and media members, most of whom are barely able to read or write in their native tongue. We are under assault by semi literates who have no respect for our history, our individual liberty, or for individual responsibilities.

Our Founding Fathers knew, understood and foresaw the probability of the eventual situation we find ourselves in today. Today, we find that there is no phase of our lives that is not subject to control by federal and/or state rules and regulations. Politicians have bought into the idea that we are unable to make decisions for ourselves and that the wisdom of this elite group is better suited to make choices for us. The steady drumbeat of our elected officials is for more control and more power over our personal affairs. We elect them to administer the government, they go to Washington and immediately begin advocating more laws that are intended to "take care of us". They become enthralled with administering our lives. They have no understanding of personal freedom and their intention is to prevent us from suffering the consequences of making poor choices by making it illegal to make a poor choice, thus becoming our "nannies".

Is this really freedom? Where is the liberty in all this?

The unintended consequences of government programs such as Social Security, the War on Poverty, Medicare, Medicaid, and the Affordable Care Act, allegedly instituted with the welfare of the people in mind, are leading to the nation's bankruptcy and loss of personal freedom. Though the path to bankruptcy is obvious, our politicians are reluctant to make hard choices that will limit or adjust these programs to save the nation because it may mean failure to be re elected. Likewise, the recipients of the programs are loath to surrender any of the benefits even if the continuation of these programs will lead to the downfall of the nation and the collapse of the economy, ending the very programs they have come to depend on.

I imagine that every day in the United States, somewhere, the topic of "What has happened to our country?" is under discussion in some form or fashion. We lament the loss of civility, the increase in crime, the breakdown of the family unit, epidemic failure of marriages, the decline of patriotism, the proliferation of unwed mothers, the failure of the work ethic, and the decline in educational standards. The general consensus of those paying attention is that our country is on the verge of a freefall into third world status while a very large segment of the population is ignorant of the predicament we are in or they just could not care less. The United States, once the greatest scientific, economic, and military juggernaut in the world and the greatest bastion of individual freedom ever known, seems to be failing.

In spite of all the problems we face the United States of America is still the last best hope for individual freedom, and for the realization of individual potential, on the planet.

Our economy is wavering on crisis; we are at war in multiple places, and our government is teetering on the edge of a slippery slope that is leading us from a representative republic to a form of government that staggers between fascism and socialism. There are no obvious leaders, at the moment, who have the honesty, integrity, courage, and faith in our form of Constitutional government, to make the tough choices necessary to restore the nation's equilibrium. Yes, we still are a powerful nation, though we have allowed the foundation of our success to be gradually eroded over the past century, we still wield a significant influence in the world. However, we are being blatantly challenged in our position as leader of the free world daily because of our growing weaknesses. The most difficult part of all of this to understand and accept is that the source of our decline comes from within. This was recognized and we were warned about it. In 1838 Abraham Lincoln said the following:

> "All the armies of Europe, Asia and Africa combined, with all the treasure of the earth (our own excepted) in their military chest; with a Bonaparte for a commander, could not by force take a drink from the Ohio, or make a track on the Blue Ridge, in a trial of a thousand years.
>
> At what point then is the approach of danger to be expected? I answer, if it ever reach us, it must spring from amongst us. It cannot come from abroad. If destruction be our lot, we must ourselves be its author and finisher. As a nation of freemen, we must live through all time, or die by suicide."

It is our own citizens: political representatives, educators, business leaders, entertainment icons and sports heroes that seem to be the most intent on destroying our culture and corrupting our history. Many of our nation's most affluent and influential men and women seem to loathe their country and display a crude, vulgar, sullen and surly disdain for the United States of America. There is a tidal wave of faithlessness that pervades the nation. Faith in anything, other than self, is met with cynicism and ridicule. Atheism has become the religion of choice for our government and apparently is becoming the choice for many of our citizens. Unfortunately, these ideologies, and attitudes are adopted and idealized by many of the best and brightest of our youth, young and impressionable as they are. As the saying goes "If you believe in nothing, you'll fall for anything."

We have been warned many times, since the founding of the United States of America that certain attitudes and actions can destroy the freedom so dearly purchased for us.

> ...*profligacy and corruption of manners make a people ripe for destruction. A good form of government may hold the rotten materials together for some time, but beyond a certain pitch, even the best constitution will be ineffectual, and slavery must ensue." —John Witherspoon, The Dominion of Providence Over the Passions of Men, 1776*

How did it happen? Who can we blame? Who is it that erodes our freedom and sells our liberty for a temporary period of pleasure, a false sense of security or a temporary position of power and influence? Who is it? I contend that a look in the mirror will reveal the culprits who have stood by and let the insanity of political correctness become the law of the land. We have stood dumbfounded as our history has been revised; our faith ridiculed; our cultural heroes reviled, and the values of the strong family unit and a close-knit community have been destroyed. We did it to ourselves. Why? It has happened because convenience has become the national idol, the cultural objective. If anything interferes with our pursuit of leisure and pleasure, it is deemed too inconvenient to be pursued.

The Culture of Convenience

We have come to loath inconvenience. If a situation requires too much involvement of our time and talent, most of us avoid it. If it can't be resolved or accomplished with a minimum of mental and physical effort, we try to find someone else to do it for us or we just circumvent the whole situation and get on with our primary objective which is personal pleasure. Entertainment is demanded in religion, education, parenting, citizenship, and self reliance. Any of the aforementioned topics must not interfere with our pursuit of leisure. Developing and organizing an idea or action that validates our personal idea of what is right and just, is now considered far too too (yes, I put it in there twice-for emphasis) time consuming. If you point out injustice applied in the name of political correctness, or condemn an aberrant behavior, you are immediately labeled as narrow minded, inconsiderate of the feelings and perspectives of your fellow human beings, too conservative, old fashioned, bigoted, strait laced, confrontational, insensitive, phobic, and on and on and on. Stand your ground and you risk the final damning labels of "hatemonger" and "racist". In addition, our culture has reverted to a cult-like worship of sexuality. The emphasis in ancient pagan religions was on the sexual aspect of every part of life, from human fertility to agricultural fertility. The value of the individual human was secondary to the worship of the sexuality of humans, animals, and deities. Has our culture devolved to the worship of sex and sexuality? Stop for a moment and think about it. Every aspect of our culture is tied to and infused with deference to youth, beauty, sexuality, and sexual expression. From entertainment to industry, the use of sex to advertise and promote is endemic. The continual emphasis on sex, sex appeal and sexuality has changed what used to be cultural norms. Relationships are no longer commitments, marriage is becoming passé`. We change partners like we change our socks, maybe more often in some cases. The quantity of sexual experiences seems to be the goal of our cultural icons. We have now reached the point at which sexual expression has been expanded to include more and more sexual aberrations. We are told that any form of sexual expression or sexual deviance is normal. If you happen to be a person of faith or just a person of a more conventional belief, you are labeled as "sexually repressive", "homophobic", a "puritan", unenlightened, regressive, or a purveyor of "hate". The expression of our ultimate devotion to sexual pleasure and convenience has an inherent problem. The problem is conception, sometimes sex results in conception, which leads to a really major inconvenience. Sex is good, child bearing is inconvenient. Sex is fun, especially sex without commitment. A child requires a long-term commitment. Sex is good; I believe that, and it is necessary, I know that. Is it the sole reason for my existence? I believed that when I was seventeen, but not now. Today, with the effectiveness and easy availability of contraceptives, unwanted pregnancy should be a rarity. However, that isn't the case. Why not? Successful contraception requires a modicum of personal responsibility. Personal responsibility interferes with the quest for "pleasure". Our culture, which once frowned on unwed childbearing, now rewards it. It is deemed cruel and unfair even to hint that getting pregnant outside of marriage may not be wise. No condemnation is allowed. Now we have baby showers in high school for expecting girls who have no husband and may have no idea exactly who the father is, but we're all just so happy for her. Why are the men automatically relieved of any responsibility for the children they have fathered? Why aren't these wayward impregnators held responsible for the children they create and dump on social services? Why is it that the rest of us must provide support with food, medicine, clothing and an education for the children they produce?

The state picks up the tab for the delivery and subsidizes the mother and child with WIC, Aid to Dependent Children, and numerous other welfare programs. So why should the young women of today worry at all about getting pregnant? Why should the father feel any responsibility for supporting his child? If all this seems just too inconvenient, there is always abortion. Just kill this one, go out, and start another one. Who cares? No charge for the abortion, that's what Social Services are for. The government will take care of you.

To be proud of the United States of America, its history, its culture, and its accomplishments is more and more considered inappropriate. I know that I'm repeating myself, but the emphasis is necessary. Defending those accomplishments, which have advanced the general welfare of humankind as a whole, will require taking a personal stand and having the knowledge to support your beliefs. If you intend to stand your ground and defend what you consider a fair and just history of this nation- be prepared. Know the history and prepare to be ridiculed and mocked. Has our generation decided that the effort and preparation required to properly defend our beliefs requires too much effort? Those who refuse to be bothered to learn the true history of their culture take refuge in ridiculing. Those who take the responsibility of learning seriously are labeled nerdy eggheads, and knowing their history makes them insensitive, intolerant, and phobic, flag-waving, uber patriots.

To know the true history of your country and to have knowledge of the actual basis of the nation's culture is vital. Education of the populace is mandatory for a strong federation of people with common values and common goals. Common values and common goals seems to advocate a "melting pot". We can't have that. However, being politically correct is so much easier and is proof that you "really care".

"I must study politics and war that my sons (and daughters*) may have liberty to study mathematics and philosophy. My sons (and daughters) *¹ ought to study mathematics and phi-losophy, geography, natural history and naval architecture, navigation, commerce and agriculture, in order to give their children a right to study painting, poetry, music, architecture, statuary, tapestry, and porcelain." —John Adams, letter to Abigail Adams, 1780

We can honor one another's beliefs and share our confidence that this nation is a source of strength and good for all. This requires that the educational system teach this nation's history honestly. Definitive study of the ideas and ideals of the founding fathers should be an in-tegral part of our institutionalized education, but it is not. Education ought to require continuing study of the Constitution.

"Every child in America should be acquainted with his own country. He should read books that furnish him with ideas that will be useful to him in life and practice. As soon as he opens his lips, he should rehearse the history of his own coun-try." —Noah Webster, On the Education of Youth in America, 1788

The truth regarding the nation's failures should not preclude con-centration on our successes. The evolving nature of our republic has continually remolded our culture and brought us through periods of discord. This was the intended goal of the Founding Fathers. Applying our Constitution was intended to bring about changes that steadi-ly produced a nation of increasingly free and productive people. However, we have strayed further and further from the Constitution, and consequently our freedoms are being severely eroded. The ide-al of limited government has slowly been replaced by a powerful, centralized government that progressively institutes more power for itself and usurps individual freedom under the guise of looking out for "the general welfare" of it citizens. Our education system has revised history and instituted a culture of self-ridicule, embarrassment and humiliation. To be proud of your American ancestry, your faith, your nation, or your history has become a point of scorn.

History has proven that a common language is a uniting characteristic. However today, enclaves of the population that have minimal interface with the nation as a whole and who through linguistic and commercial separation cultivate isolationism, induce animosity and promote alienation between groups. Groups that should have assimilated into the culture, should have become fluent in the English language, should have integrated into the economic and political structure of the nation, instead have become hostile islands of people loyal to their nation of origin while rejecting the country and culture they live in.

> *At one time, immigrants came to America to become Americans. Today, the apostles of multiculturalism and grievance-mongering have done their best to keep foreigners foreign and, if possible, feeling aggrieved. Our own schools and colleges teach grievances. —Thomas Sowell*

Under the dictates of "political correctness", new citizens are urged to insulate and isolate themselves; to retain their native language, their cultural identity, and to advocate non-assimilation. Retention of cultural identity and language is fine and admirable, but not at the expense of national unity.

The racist in me: In 1960, while stationed with the Marines at Kaneohe Marine Corps Air Station, First Battalion, 4th Marines, Fourth Marine Brigade, Charlie Company, a conversation with a group of Marines turned to the topic of our sergeants.

I mentioned a Gunnery Sergeant who often walked around without his boots on.

15

Apparently no one knew who I was talking about and I was asked to describe him. "He's the tall, black, gunny in Bravo Company." This met with a stony silence and then one of the black Marines informed me that I had just made a racist statement. He informed me that the gunny was a Negro, not a Black. I was then interrogated as to where I came from and why I would say something like that. Having been properly chastised I apologized confirming that I had meant nothing derogatory by the statement.

Not long after that the term "Negro" become verboten. Now it was perfectly acceptable to refer to Americans of African descent as "black". I adjusted, learning the dance of interracial relations.

A few years later, I was in a night class taking African American History. Now it was truly racist to mention blacks or Negroes. No, now we (white Americans) were to refer to our black peers as "African Americans".

By this time, I had matured enough to begin making observations of the different cultural machinations that were occurring all around me. It had become acceptable for my African American peers to refer to me as "honkey", "whitey", "redneck", or "cracker" and to my entire race as "racist bigots" and to each other with the horrific "n" word, without a hint of resistance or offense from the mainstream movers and shakers of the culture. My brothers and sisters and I, who were born with pale skin short of the melanin to make us dark enough to be "hip", "cool", to have "soul", were constantly on the defensive trying to assure the world that we weren't racists. Everything involving personal relationships between individuals was initially established by the color of our skin. What we believed; what we stood for, honor, integrity, all were secondary considerations. First and foremost, relationships were based on skin color. I finally realized that Martin Luther King, Jr. had failed to fully impress his message on his own.

*"I have a dream that my four little children will one day live
in a nation where they will not be judged by the color of their
skin, but by the content of their character."* —M.L. King, Jr.

I'm sure that he intended for that to apply to all races as they related
to one another. Why? Because he also said *"I have a dream that one
day on the red hills of Georgia, the sons of former slaves and the sons
of former slave owners will be able to sit together at the table of broth-
erhood..."* —M.L. King, Jr.

It is not happening.

The Unmentionable Invasion

It cannot be denied that our nation is under assault by an invasion of immigrants who are bypassing the admittedly convoluted legal path provided for entering, working in, and becoming a citizen of the United States. We have students attending our schools who are applauded for taking down the national flag in front of the school and running the flag of Mexico up in its place.[2] While our national holidays receive minimal recognition, Cinco de Mayo, a day hardly noticed in Mexico is a cause célèbre in the United States. Our schools in many areas are required to teach in primary languages other than English.[3] English is taught as the secondary language.[4] In southern Florida and areas of our southwestern states the common language in the streets is not English. Our elections are fraught with illegal immigrants voting politicians into office who are sympathetic to their cause. These illegal immigrants have no right to vote, but there is no concerted effort to prevent their voting. In fact, many of our politicians actively solicit their vote.[5] If you, or I, speak up and demand that this issue be addressed the immediate response is that we are racists. We are accused of trying to subvert the opportunities of minorities. The fact that they are illegal and have no right to vote in our elections is not relevant. The fact that these folks are loyal to their homeland and have no affinity or appreciation of the United States or its laws seems to be of no consequence. Apparently, common sense has little weight, as our nation seems to be hell bent on self-destruction.

Theodore Roosevelt's ideas on Immigrants and being an AMERICAN in 1907.

'In the first place, we should insist that if the immigrant who comes here in good faith becomes an American and assimilates himself to us, he shall be treated on an exact equality with everyone else, for it is an outrage to discriminate against any such man because of creed, or birthplace, or origin. But this is predicated upon the person's becoming in every facet an American, and nothing but an American...There can be no divided allegiance here. Any man who says he is an American, but something else also, isn't an American at all. We have room for but one flag, the American flag... We have room for but one language here, and that is the English language... And we have room for but one sole loyalty and that is a loyalty to the American people.'

Moral, Immoral, Amoral?

Morality has been thrown overboard; not just individual morality but cultural morality. Individuals have been groomed by our educational system and our media centered information system to tolerate any conduct or behavior except those that disagree with their own acceptance of rude, crude, and amoral speech or activity. Disagreement with the progressive liberal opinion will not be tolerated.

Our entertainment media flaunts immorality through television, movies, and literature. Graphic sex and sexuality are commonplace in all of our entertainment media. Marital fidelity is rarely, if ever, the norm in the portrayal of families. Profanity has become mandatory in all forms of media. Radio, TV, film, and the written media are all resplendent with cursing, and the mighty "F... bomb" is bandied about by all. Teenagers, politicians, actors, actresses, lords and ladies find no fault with the most profane language imaginable. It is a sign of open mindedness, of being hip; proof that you are not a prude. Our government officials, elected and appointed, and civil servants, local as well as state and federal, have embraced the language and actions of immorality. The multitude of "open mike" episodes reveals that those in positions of influence who were once expected to conduct themselves in a moral and just manner have chosen to "get down" with the prevailing degradation of the culture. At one time, not so long ago, they were to serve as an example of honor and integrity for the community and the nation. They didn't always measure up to expectations, but the expectation was there never the less. Today our politicians are among the most blatant offenders as far as morality goes. They lie under oath, they cheat, they misappropriate, and mislead. Even when the general public is aware of their shenanigans, the incumbents are routinely re elected. Why? Because our culture has become so jaded regarding right and wrong, what is just and unjust, that we actually expect to find our leaders to be amoral. We make excuses for their failures and there are rarely sincere demands that they correct their behavior or that they suffer any consequences for their actions. The current mantra is that "their immoral behavior in their private life has nothing to do with and no effect on their ability to govern".

> *"We have no government armed with power capable of contending with human passions unbridled by morality and religion. Avarice, ambition, revenge, or gallantry, would break the strongest cords of our Constitution as a whale goes through a net. Our Constitution was made only for a moral and religious people. It is wholly inadequate to the government of any other." —John Adams, Address to the Military, 1798*

The recent demands for the cessation of all incidents of sexual harassment and that the perpetrators of past sexual misconduct be brought to justice is a good thing. However I see no reason to stop at "sexual harassment". There are other violations of moral conduct that ought to be equally brought to light and proper consequences applied.

Maybe we have come to believe that the rules of moral conduct apply only to the common folks and are no longer appropriate for the elite class. Who are the elites?

You name them, we know who they are. Many are elected, many are exceptionally wealthy, many are exceptionally talented...and many obviously consider themselves "elite" and "above the law" and we allow them to do so.

We Are "The Government"

The contention that the Constitution no longer meets the needs of the nation is the result of the moral decline of our culture. The truth is that "We the people" no longer fit the Constitution. It is not that the Constitution no longer works or can work, it is that we cannot function within its boundaries because it requires a fine sense of individual freedom, individual responsibility and a defined set of rules regarding the limits on the power of government. We are no longer willing to define what is right or wrong. The failure is rampant through every segment of the population; every branch of government. Stop and recall the news reports exposing presidents, governors, senators, representatives, and judges whose behavior has violated not only the law, but also the universal sense of what is morally just.

Judges and lawyers in general need to understand the difference between the law and the intent of the law. We the people need to understand the difference between the law and the intent of the law. Laws are supposed to be the way a civilized society assures that justice is done in every case. The laws are supposed to keep civilization civil. When the application of the law results in injustice, a judge is expected to "judge" the situation and render a "just" decision. Measures need to be instituted to revise the ineffective laws to mitigate the unintended consequences. We often find our judges shrugging their shoulders at obvious injustice and telling us "It's the law and it has to be enforced." or on the other hand ignoring the law altogether "for the general good of the people" because it is politically incorrect. Rather than institute the necessary changes they take the easy way out.

Often the law is contorted and blatantly convoluted to disguise its misuse to meet a particular political or economic preference. We, using common sense, understand that it's all often written to cater to a particular political or economic interest. Whether it is written to institute universal justice is irrelevant. Rather than demand correction we wring our hands in disgust and then head for the golf course or Disney World, or to the sports arena to be entertained. It takes too much time and effort to challenge the legal mumbo jumbo engaged in by lawyers, judges and politicians to justify their ridiculous decisions. It is obviously not their purpose to assure that what is right and just is the result of their actions. So, what is the point? Obviously, we really don't want to know.

It seems that very few, among those in authority, can boast that they strive to maintain a decent level of morality. I should rephrase that. They all assure us that they are truly doing the peoples business in a just and moral fashion.

> *"Public virtue cannot exist in a nation without private, and public virtue as the only foundation of republics. There must be a positive passion for the public good, the public interest, honor, power and glory, established in the minds of the people, or there can be no republican government, nor any real liberty: and this public passion must be superior to all private passions." —John Adams, letter to Mercy Warren, 1776*

As I said before, when the population as a whole has made its preference for pleasure and convenience manifest, the politicians are sure to follow. The public knows when they are having a large dose of manure shoveled at them, what is unsettling is their general ambivalence.

Who Are We Electing?

The present situation we find our nation in speaks volumes about those who have been governing. No member of either political party is exempted from using their position for personal gain. The longer they stay in power the more subject to corruption they become. The old adage, "Power corrupts and absolute power corrupts absolutely" is not a figment of some idealist's imagination. It is truth in action.

Whether in politics or in carrying out of the business of producing goods and services, what is reasonable and just no longer seems to be a priority. Whether you are a politician or part of the labor force or a member of management within a large corporation, the primary objective is to exert as little as possible and get as much as possible without regard to quality. That has almost become the universally accepted standard, in unions, corporations, and small businesses and with private individuals. Getting the most for the least is not just an economic perspective; it has become the mandatory ideology of the culture. Pride in a job well done has been replaced by "get the most reward for the least effort regardless of the quality of the product". There is a right and just way to conduct business that will result in a reasonable profit. A quality product produced by quality labor receiving a fair wage can produce, not just adequate, but exceptional products. Pride in workmanship is becoming more and more rare.

How We Got Here

The age of enlightenment culminated in 1776 when a collection of the finest minds of the age gathered in Philadelphia and brought to fruition the ideal of individual freedom and personal responsibility. They ignited the flame that would enlighten the world. The great experience of self government had begun. Seed that had been planted during the renaissance and nurtured by the likes of Hume and Locke germinated in the minds of those who formed the Continental Congress. Madison, Jefferson, Adams, Franklin, Hancock, Henry, Paine, Hamilton and all those representing the various colonies produced the Declaration of Independence and subsequently the Constitution of the United States of America.

When delivered to the British authorities a cover letter by John Hancock, dated July 6, 1776, was attached to our Declaration of Independence.

> "Gentlemen, Altho it is not possible to forsee the consequences of human actions, yet it is nevertheless a duty we owe ourselves and posterity in all our public councils to decide in the best manner we are able and to trust the event to That Being who governs both causes and events, so as to bring about His own determinations. Impressed with this sentiment, and at the same time fully convinced that our affairs will take a more favorable turn, The

> *Congress have judged it necessary to dissolve all connection*
> *between Great Britain and the American Colonies, and to de-*
> *clare them free and independent States as you will perceive*
> *by the enclosed Declaration, which I am directed to transmit*
> *to you."*

In conclusion, each of the signers vowed their personal commitment to the endeavor they had begun.

> *"For the support of this declaration, with the firm reliance on*
> *the protection of the Divine Providence, we mutually pledge*
> *to each other our lives, our fortunes, and our sacred honor."*

They took that vow seriously and most of them suffered dearly for standing by that vow.

What were the mutually held values that brought these men together to embark on an endeavor that would culminate in the founding of the United States of America?

They acknowledged that certain actions initiate a duty to respond. These founders had an acute awareness that individual actions have personal consequences. They possessed faith in something or someone greater than themselves, they believed in a just and moral government, and the right of the individual to be free and independent.

What they produced acknowledged the supreme value of the individual to have an undeniable right to live his or her life in the most earnest pursuit of life, liberty, and happiness; that a citizen could accomplish all that they had the ability and the desire to accomplish; that the state had very limited claims on a citizen's time and talent.

That awareness held these men together in a common cause. Such beliefs still flicker in the hearts of some of us today.

Who in the political arena today will commit their all to the preservation of the country and our culture? Think carefully. Remember all those in positions of leadership who haven't ducked and run when it came time to put their personal wealth and position at risk. Who among us stands in defiance of the absurdity of political correctness and in the face of accusations of being "old fashioned", "out of touch", "religious fanatics", or "racist hate mongers"? It's now much more acceptable to pack up and shut up than to stand up for what you believe in and risk losing position and possessions.

> *"I love the man that can smile in trouble, that can gather strength from distress, and grow brave by reflection. 'Tis the business of little minds to shrink; but he whose heart is firm, and whose conscience approves his conduct, will pursue his principles unto death."* —Thomas Paine

> *"Our future lies not in the size of government, but in the people who drive this country's prosperity: the entrepreneurs, the innovators, and those who work hard to achieve their American Dream."* –Congressman Rob Wittman (2010 News letter)

A number of our elected officials have committed nothing to the nation. They are beholden to corporate donors, wealthy supporters, and their political party. These all come before the welfare of the nation as a whole. Many have never served in the military and have no loyalty to anything that isn't primarily beneficial to themselves.

We have an obligation to stand up for our nation and our culture. We have our faults, but the contributions that we, as a nation, have made to improve the lives of people throughout the world are too magnificent to ignore. So be proud and speak up. Stand up for yourselves, be proud to be a patriot. Let the sullen, surly, sarcastic, libertines who assault you and your faith, your country, and your culture know that you have turned the other cheek for the last time. The progressives in this world have been striving to make The United States of America the doormat for the world to wipe its feet on for over a century now. Its time for resistance to take hold, and because America is a nation of justice and high ideals we must prevail.

Good, Bad, or Indifferent?

The generosity of the citizens of the United States rarely enjoys the sustained focus of either the media or our educational institutions. After every natural disaster, whether a hurricane, earthquake, drought, or political upheaval, the American people step up and give from their hearts. Millions of dollars in aid are funneled to areas and countries that are in distress.

A hurricane tears through Central America. Civil war creates refugees in the Balkans. Famine strikes the Horn of Africa. Two decades of war in Afghanistan its new government unable to deliver the most basic of services. In these and other situations around the world, the compassion of the American people goes pouring out to those in need through USAID.

The United States gives more to those in crises than any other country in the world. USAID is the U.S. Government agency that is responsible for directing these contributions to thousands of non-profit partners and international organizations like the World Food Program and UNICEF. In tandem with these organizations, the agency helps those affected by disaster to cope and then begin again by converting crisis situations into opportunities to promote peace, democracy, and economic growth. USAID ensures that all of this assistance is spent in the way that most effectively helps those who are in need. —http://www.usaid.gov.

For a nation to be able to "give" it first has to "have". America gives out of its abundance, which is the result of freedom, the freedom to pursue life, liberty, and happiness and the cultural value placed on the individual right to own property. It is amazing that the largess poured out by the United States to the world provides sustenance to governments and cultures that despise the United States and actively attack our people and our beliefs.

A Better Way?

Beginning in the early 20th century the "progressive" label has become almost sacred. The objective of those who claim to be progressives is a utopia that is impossible to achieve in a free society. Forced equality of outcome "to each according to their needs, from each according to their ability" is only possible under an unconditional dictatorship. I'm sorry if that offends you. Equality of outcome is an elusive goal. We can all start at the starting line, but some one individual will cross the finish line first. The rest of us will cross according to our ability and how much initiative we're willing to expend. The dream of a world where everyone is equally endowed with stuff and everyone is satisfied with the stuff they have is just that, a dream.

There has never been a nation where everyone is in charge, and no one is responsible; where all were achieving exactly what everyone feels is fair. A nation where everyone works together for the same reward, regardless of time or talent expended, and they all agree that this is fair, does not exist, never has existed. Utopia only exists in the minds of those who envy what others have. Utopians want to have everything they desire but with minimal exertion on their part to achieve those desires. They are perfectly happy to let others exert themselves, especially when the workers have to share their achievements with those who are reapers not sowers. You know, it's not fair that some have more than others even though they to put forth more effort. After all, we're all human beings; don't we deserve to have all that we desire? That appears to be what we have come to consider equality. If you dare to assert that all are not guaranteed a life of equal results without regard to qualifications or abilities you will suffer the slings and arrows of those who insist that equal opportunity must result in equal accomplishment. The relationship between effort, merit, reward, and success, seems to have been forgotten.

> *"To take from one, because it is thought his own industry and that of his fathers has acquired too much, in order to spare to others, who, or whose fathers, have not exercised equal industry and skill, is to violate arbitrarily the first principle of association, the guarantee to everyone the free exercise of his industry and the fruits acquired by it." —Thomas Jefferson*

If we just look at the whole idea of a utopian socialist or communist ideal (progressive), and if we are honest with ourselves, we know we're not going to work so that our neighbor can have a big screen TV just like ours whether he works for it or not. We know that in a society where everyone is equal, there are always those running the equality who consider themselves to be "more equal" than everybody else. Take notice that the "progressives" who are extremely wealthy are not striving to make everyone as wealthy as they are. No, what they want is for everyone else to "share their wealth" and understand that they, being in charge, deserve to have more because they're the "progressive leaders". You must recognize that these "progressives" are making sure that you get your fair share of the product of everyone else's labor and that their fair share is far greater than everyone else's because they are "the leaders". The leaders are entitled to more because? Well of course they deserve more because they are taking care of all the rest of us and making sure that we all have the same amount of stuff and that it's all the same kind of stuff. They will be assuring us that all are doing equal amounts of labor for the stuff they are making sure we get. It's very simple, if you're a leader you deserve more stuff and better stuff. Take a close look at the leaders of the progressive movement. They seem to be doing pretty well compared to the folks they are leading. Do they really believe that they deserve more and the rest of us should have equal shares of what's left? Come on folks!! It really is time to take off the rose-colored glasses and look at the world as it is. The truth is that those who are smarter, who work harder and longer, will have more. Paradise on earth may come, but it won't come at our hands.

1. You cannot legislate the poor into prosperity, by legislating the wealthy out of prosperity.

2. What one person receives without working for, another person must work for without receiving.

3. The government cannot give to anybody anything that the government does not first take from somebody else.

4. You cannot multiply wealth by dividing it.

5. *When half of the people get the idea that they do not have to work because the other half is going to take care of them, and when the other half gets the idea that it does no good to work, because somebody else is going to get what they work for, that is the beginning of the end of any nation. —Author Unknown*

Who Is Responsible?

Today we find that we have surrendered most personal decisions to the state. Why?

Our focus has been shifted from guarding our individual freedom to indulging our personal pleasure. The founding fathers took for granted that people would take personal responsibility for insuring individual freedom. Individual rights and personal freedom were important. Responsibility and duty were understood to be part and parcel of everyone's life. It wasn't the State's responsibility to provide for your personal freedom, it was your responsibility to prevent the State from encroaching on your freedom by usurping your responsibility. Today we have no interest in the activities of our political leaders if it interferes in any way with our quest for the ultimate entertainment. If the choice is to attend a meeting with your congressman or go to a concert with the latest music icon, there is no contest. The congressman will have a sparse audience and the concert will be sold out. The business of government cannot compete with NASCAR, the NFL, American Idol, or Dancing with the Stars. Today the vast majority of our citizens have no idea who their senator or representative is. They can give you intimate details of personal history and current love life of their favorite movie stars, sports figures, music sensations, and any others who make up the "rich and famous" of the entertainment world. When challenged regarding their lack of political awareness you are usually met with a shrug and "I don't do politics."

- *Just because you do not take an interest in politics doesn't mean politics won't take an interest in you! Pericles (430 B.C.)*

- *One of the penalties of not participating in politics is that you will be governed by your inferiors." Plato*

- *"No people will tamely surrender their liberties, nor can any be easily subdued, when knowledge is diffused and virtue is preserved. On the contrary, when people are universally ignorant, and debauched in their manners, they will sink under their own weight without the aid of foreign Invaders." —Samuel Adams, letter to James Warren, 1775*

What has happened that has brought us to the state of affairs that "we the people" find ourselves in today?

There was a time, not so long ago, when people took pride in their country, their history, the culture of the United States, and in the work they accomplished. There was a time in the not too distant past that a man's goal was to succeed in providing for himself and for his family; that time has been swept away in a tide of history revision, self indulgence, and rejection of the basic building blocks that made the United States and its citizens the envy of the entire world.

"Today, we tend to think of John D. Rockefeller as just one of those famous rich people. But Rockefeller didn't just 'happen to have money.' How he got rich is the real story—and it is a story whose implications reach far beyond that one particular individual. Before Rockefeller's innovations reduced the price of kerosene to a fraction of what it had once been, there wasn't a lot for poor people to do when nightfall came, other than go to bed. But the advent of cheap kerosene added hours of light and activity to each day for people with low or

35

moderate incomes. ... Henry Ford's mass production methods cut in half the cost of producing the famous Model T Ford in just five years. People who had once lived their entire lives within a narrow radius of a relatively few miles could now go see places they never knew about before. ... Today we seldom even know the names of those who have made monumental contributions to human well-being. All we know is that some people have gotten 'rich' and that this is to be regarded as some sort of grievance. Many of the people we honor today are people who are skilled in the rhetoric of grievances and promises of new 'rights' at someone else's expense. But is that what is going to make a better America?" —economist Thomas Sowell

A large segment of our population is infused, by the educational system and cultural icons as well as our government, with a loathing of idea of success through personal responsibility and effort. Now our schools teach that our ancestors were evil, that every step of progress and every success of the nation has been achieved through deceit, deception, and fraud. The most despised are those who were once our heroes. From Christopher Columbus to the Founding Fathers, there is not an honorable human in the bunch according to our history revisionists. If you were a European you are especially despicable. The Spanish, Portuguese, English, French, and German explorers have been maligned by our academic elite for the past hundred years.

If a moment or two is expended carefully evaluating who we are and where we came from, you can deduce for yourselves that most of our modern education regarding history and culture are imposed to emphasize the negative and minimize the positive. That is not to propose that there were no, and are no, events in our history that should not be pointed out as mistakes; wrong from their inception to their fruition. But the result of recent history revision has been to instill guilt and self loathing in our people. It is difficult to find institutions of higher learning that teach that although the United States has dark episodes in its history, it has accomplished much more that is good for it's people and for the people of all nations. The United States must be recognized as having led the world into an era of freedom and prosperity unimagined by those pilgrims who first landed on our shores.

So, what happened? What led The United States, this destination of immigrants, to fall from being the bastion of hope and freedom to being considered, even by many of its own citizens, as the source of all that is wrong in the world?

It seems to have begun when the idea that everyone should have the basics of food, clothing, and shelter provided without cost to, or effort from, themselves. In the beginning, this idea was intended to apply to those who could not, due to physical or mental inability, or temporary misfortune, provide for themselves.

This is indeed a noble and a right idea and should be the objective of all societies. However, as time passed, the ideal changed. It became the right of "everyone" regardless of their effort or ability, to be furnished with food, clothing, and shelter and entertainment. The guidelines changed from "to each according to their needs" to "to each according to their wants". Then the question is "who decides what wants must be provided?"

When the definition of "needs" was expanded to include "wants", the responsibility of just who was to supply these basic needs or wants was easy. Those who work the hardest, and have acquired the most, they have more than enough and should be obligated to provide for those in need. At first, the inclination is that this is all right. If all who worked chipped in a bit, the few who couldn't work would be taken care of. It all seemed reasonable and "fair". The naïve assumption of most is that those who can work will work. The truth though is that every culture and every society have a segment of the population that has no desire to work. These folks are especially loath to work if they can get what they want without effort. When they learn that they can manipulate the system to progress from providing basic needs to including many of their "wants" as well, it is utopia!!

We have fostered a large segment of our population who take pride in being able to "work" the system. They have learned to provide for themselves and for their families at their neighbor's expense. These neighbors who apply their time and talent to support themselves and pay their taxes, fund the government that provides programs supporting the social feeding trough.

Who Will Be Responsible?

We have come to demand that government take the responsibility for everything that requires a choice that supports our health and well being. We don't want to be bothered with difficulties of providing for our own basic needs. Food, shelter, and health needs have been deemed too problematic for us. Pursuit of the basic needs of life interferes with our pursuit of pleasure and entertainment.

This is a manifestation of the before mentioned advent of very little pride in a job well done. The point of pride these days seems to be how little we had to do to receive an unearned benefit; a benefit that we have become proud to have someone else foot the bill for. We call it "free" when it doesn't appear to cost us money out of our own pocket. We have forgotten the adage "nothing is free'. Someone pays for every aspect of our survival. There really are no "free rides". If it doesn't come directly out of your pocket then someone else is footing the bill for you.

We have convinced our government to pay our way by forcing the taxpayers to pick up the tab. The taxpayer is the victim that the government fleeces at the point of a gun. You have no say over how the money, pilfered from your paycheck before you ever see it, is spent. Try to refuse to pay your taxes and the wrath of the IRS will descend on you, armed to the teeth, and indignant that you would dare to have the audacity to resist. Money is taken from you to support programs that usurp your freedom and is used to reward the "less fortunate" who have learned how to extract a substantial lifestyle by manipulating the system. If you protest you are immediately labeled with any number of derogatory titles. To merely ask for accountability for the use of the money you provide engenders you being labeled as selfish, greedy, hatemonger, racist, homophobe, fascist, Nazi, and insensitive to the needs of others. You, as the provider of the funds, have only one purpose. You are to provide the wherewithal to sustain a growing culture of parasites, and shut up.

There is no respect from either your government or your neighbors for being the source of their plenty. There is no glory in being independent. There is little desire to ensure personal freedom. True freedom demands self sufficiency. Every responsibility we hand off to "the government" is a surrender of our freedom. Bit by bit and piece by piece, we have surrendered our independence and freedom for convenience.

To Be or Not to Be, Responsible.

We want the state to raise our children. We want to send our children to school for state provided breakfast, lunch and then into a state funded after school program that provides supper. In addition, we would hope that the school will teach them to read, write, add and subtract. However, only after they are provided with a keen appreciation for the protection provided by the state to prevent parental discipline, an enduring dependence on the government for all of their basic needs, sex education and birth control, and the acute environmental awareness that human beings are destroying the earth. Parents have, for all intents, surrendered their parental responsibilities to the state. Actually, they didn't "surrender" these responsibilities; it appears that they could not wait to dump the whole family responsibility thing onto the shoulders of the state.

> "It is the duty of parents to maintain their children decently, and according to their circumstances; to protect them according to the dictates of prudence; and to educate them according to the suggestions of a judicious and zealous regard for their usefulness, their respectability and happiness."
> – James Wilson, Lectures on Law, 1791

> "[T]he only foundation for a useful education in a republic is to be laid in religion. Without this there can be no virtue, and without virtue there can be no liberty, and liberty is the object

and life of all republican governments." —Benjamin Rush, On the Mode of Education Proper in a Republic, 1806

The family unit has been destroyed by our local, state, and federal government taking control and implementing law that intrudes into every aspect of our personal lives.[6] It has been destroyed by the attitude that child rearing requires at least a masters degree, preferably a PhD. After all, child rearing is soooo inconvenient and to have all the stuff we want in this unfair society both parents have to work so we will be able to have it all. Stuff is what is important!! Family? Family is such an old-fashioned idea. This attitude has resulted in our local, state, and federal government taking control and implementing law that intrudes into, not only parenting, but into every aspect of our personal lives.

> *"When the family fails, the economy suffers and social pathologies ensue. This invites government intervention, which contracts liberty.... The federal government's programs are no substitute for a mom and a dad in the home. The hard data demonstrates that all children living in intact homes do better in school—and this costs taxpayers nothing extra. ...What right is more important than the right to life? If we cannot be secure in our persons, will we remain long secure in our property? ... The family that remains together—and that worships regularly—can point the path to society's renewal. ... The fiscal costs of social breakdown are massive. Fewer people mean a weaker economy: It has been estimated that since 1970, abortion has cost the nation a minimum of $35 trillion. And government pays hugely for pathologies that derive from broken families and broken lives." —Tony Perkins, President of Family Research Council*

We don't want to be bothered with making judgments on anything. We want the rules to be written out for us and then we can apply the rules as they are written without having to put any thought into the application. We don't want to be bothered with considering the intent of the law or the unintended consequences. Our primary concern appears to be complying with the letter of the law. To consider the "intent" requires the application of common sense, a bit of deductive reasoning, and that poses an inconvenience. It's so much easier to just read the rules and apply them as written. How can you be judged wrong if you comply with the letter of the law? After all, you didn't make the rules, you are just supposed to abide by them, which endorses government enforcement. Right? What should happen? When the letter of the law is obviously contrary to what was intended to be the result, then the law ought to be changed expeditiously. Not just left hanging there with its unintended consequences accumulating.

Our schools have become mini prisons. Why? We have forsaken imposing any discipline on our children. Discipline and child abuse have become the same thing in the eyes of the state and many parents. It is easier to make blanket rules than to seek out and punish the real offenders. Child abusers should be punished. Children require discipline. There is nothing so pathetic as watching parents trying to use reason and logic to persuade a three-year-old that what the child is doing is wrong. Parents are not allowed to engage in corporal punishment. Parents refuse to allow the teachers to enforce any discipline on their children. Under no circumstance is our child to be made to feel ashamed of their words or actions. Shame is not to be tolerated.

Therefore, we have the children, in all their infinite wisdom, in charge of the school and the home environment. We are obstinate in our demand that children be allowed to express themselves. The result is that we have young thugs who terrorize the teachers as well as their fellow students. They are rude, vulgar, and absolutely in opposition to all authority. Remember, we were all opposed to authority when we were their age, but our parents let us know, in no uncertain terms, who was in authority. Now we stand on the sidelines wringing our hands and whining that "the government ought to do something about the chaos in our schools." Friends, we are the government!!

> *"I know no safe depository of the ultimate powers of the society but the people themselves; and if we think them not enlightened enough to exercise their control with a wholesome discretion, the remedy is not to take it from them, but to inform their discretion by education. This is the true corrective of abuses of constitutional power." —Thomas Jefferson, letter to William Charles Jarvis, 1820*

Attempts to restore some vestige of control gave rise to the "zero tolerance" mantra. Of course, imposing zero tolerance requires the school administrator to implement the program. Unfortunately, our current crop of administrators is the culmination of a generation that has been educated and matured under the government directed education system. Common sense? No chance!! Zero tolerance disallows any accidents. Every occurrence must be perpetrated by a person and that person must be held responsible. Let's see how the "zero tolerance" program is administered:

CNSNews.com, Tuesday, March 27, 2001

> *A picture of a soldier holding a canteen and a knife has earned the third-grade boy who drew it a suspension from school.*

> *Wire reports said the third-grader also drew a fort, listing its inventory as guns, knives and first-aid kits.*

> *The principal of Lenwill Elementary School in West Monroe, La., is quoted as saying that the school "can't tolerate anything that has to do with guns or knives." According to press reports, school officials stand by their decision to punish the child for "a violent arrangement."*

The boy's father said he was forced to explain to his son that being in the Army and owning guns "is not bad."

This is obviously "zero tolerance" run amuck.

Model Student, Sports Star Suspended for Paring Knife Mix-Up, December 29, 2010 — by Bryan Preston

On its face, this looks like it's an asinine decision which is probably the product of a culture that makes lawsuits possible in every action we take. How else to explain what the school principal has done here? It's either the school's fear of a lawsuit, or a total lack of common sense among the school's leadership, or there's something we don't know about all this that hasn't shown up in the media reports. I'm not discounting that third possibility, but based on what we know from media reports, this is indefensible: An athletic and academic standout in Lee County said a lunchbox mix-up has cut short her senior year of high school and might hurt her college opportunities. Ashley Smithwick, 17, of Sanford, was suspended from Southern Lee High School in October after school personnel found a small paring knife in her lunchbox. Smithwick said personnel found the knife while searching the belongings of several students, possibly looking for drugs.

"She got pulled into it. She doesn't have to be a bad person to be searched," Smithwick's father, Joe Smithwick, said. The lunchbox really belonged to Joe Smithwick, who packs a paring knife to slice his apple. He and his daughter have matching lunchboxes. "It's just an honest mistake. That was supposed to be my lunch because it was a whole apple," he said. Not only has Smithwick never been in trouble before, she has been taking college courses in advance of her high school graduation, indicating that she's smart and responsible. Throw in the

45

soccer skills, and she may be a lock for scholarships, and this suspension with the accompanying media attention obviously jeopardizes that.

News accounts all focus on the school superintendent, Jeff Moss, but by his own statement he didn't actually make the decision here. School principal Bonnie Almond, who doesn't show up in any of the news stories that I ran across, is the decider. Darla Cole, the chief school resource officer in Lee County, told WRAL News she could not comment on the case.

Lee County Superintendent Jeff Moss told the Sanford Herald that he can't discuss the specifics of the case, but school policy allows principals to consider the context of each case and determine discipline.

Moss said students who accidentally carry a weapon and report it to teachers will get a light punishment. If teachers find it, he said, the discipline is harsher.

So going by all that and the known facts in this case, if Smithwick had told the searcher about the knife ahead of time she would still have been punished, but lightly. Mitigating circumstance: Smithwick had no idea that the knife was in her lunchbox. She was evidently as surprised as anyone when it turned up. This demands ruining her senior year and jeopardizing her higher ed?

The Virginia Gazette, Williamsburg, Virginia-February 27, 2002

(An excerpt from an article regarding the history of "Zero Tolerance" in schools)

*But the application of the code in cases of bullying is trou-
blesome, since it disallows self-defense. Hence, the bullied
student has no recourse other than to, as Maranzano says,
run away from the conflict and seek the help of the nearest
adult – an option that, for image-building middle and high
school students under constant peer pressure, seems totally
unrealistic. Consequently, the student who reaches his limits
of toleration and finally strikes back at the bully is, under the
zero toleration code, just as subject to being handcuffed and
escorted off the premises as the bully. As a middle school parent whose son has been the object of bullying, told me, "the
[zero tolerance] policies seem to ignore the factors that lead
to conflict. The result is not that conflict is suppressed, but it is
now expressed in insults rather than overt aggression. The kid
with a mean mouth is king."*

This is a fine reflection on the state of our education system. Those
who are supposed to be teaching young people how to cope with the
world they are growing up in, appear to be acting like idiots. Placed
in positions of authority they are unable to understand or apply the
intent of the rule versus applying the rules literally. The excuse offered
is that they are "not authorized" to "interpret" the rules. Parents are
equally at fault because in our litigious society parents are quick to
sue at any perceived encroachment on their child's person, or failure
on the part of the school to implement these ridiculous rules. Why
pass up an opportunity to glean a small fortune from the situation?

The following is alleged to be the introduction speech delivered by
a new principal to his staff and student body. It probably earned him
a reprimand from the school board. Even though it is right in every
aspect, it might have cost him his job.

*"I am your new principal, and honored to be so. There is no
greater calling than to teach young people. I would like to ap-*

prise you of some important changes coming to our school. I am making these changes because I am convinced that most of the ideas that have dominated public education in America have worked against you, against your teachers and against our country.

First, this school will no longer honor race or ethnicity. I could not care less if your racial makeup is black, brown, red, yellow or white. I could not care less if your origins are African, Latin American, Asian or European, or if your ancestors arrived here on the Mayflower or on slave ships. The only identity I care about, the only one this school will recognize, is your individual identity—your character, your scholarship, your humanity. And the only national identity this school will care about is American.

This is an American public school, and American public schools were created to make better Americans. If you wish to affirm an ethnic, racial or religious identity through school, you will have to go elsewhere. We will end all ethnicity, race and un-American nationality-based celebrations. They undermine the motto of America, one of its three central values—e pluribus Unum, "from many, one."

And this school will be guided by America's values. This includes all after-school clubs. I will not authorize clubs that divide students based on any identities.

This includes race, language, religion, sexual orientation or whatever else may become in vogue in a society divided by political correctness.

Your clubs will be based on interests and passions, not blood, ethnic, racial or other physically defined ties. Those clubs just cultivate narcissism—an unhealthy preoccupation with the self—while the purpose of education is to get you to think beyond yourself. So, we will have clubs that transport you to the wonders and glories of art, music, astronomy, languages you do not already speak, carpentry and more. If the only extracurricular activities you can imagine being interested in are those based on ethnic, racial or sexual identity, that means that little outside of yourself really interests you.

Second, I am uninterested in whether English is your native language. My only interest in terms of language is that you leave this school speaking and writing English as fluently as possible. The English language has united America's citizens for over 200 years, and it will unite us at this school. It is one of the indispensable reasons this country of immigrants has always come to be one country.

And if you leave this school without excellent English language skills, I would be remiss in my duty to ensure that you will be prepared to successfully compete in the American job market. We will learn other languages here—it is deplorable that most Americans only speak English —but if you want classes taught in your native language rather than in English, this is not your school.

Third, because I regard learning as a sacred endeavor, everything in this school will reflect learning's elevated status. This means, among other things, that you and your teachers will dress accordingly.

Many people in our society dress more formally for Hollywood events than for church or school. These people have their priorities backward. Therefore, there will be a formal dress code at this school.

Fourth, no obscene language will be tolerated anywhere on this school's property—whether in class, in the hallways or at athletic events. If you can't speak without using the f-word, you can't speak. By obscene language I mean the words banned by the Federal Communications Commission, plus epithets such as "Nigger," even when used by one black student to address another black, or "bitch," even when addressed by a girl to a girlfriend. It is my intent that by the time you leave this school, you will be among the few your age to instinctively distinguish between the elevated and the degraded, the holy and the obscene.

Fifth, we will end all self-esteem programs. In this school, self-esteem will be attained in only one way—the way people attained it until decided otherwise a generation ago—by earning it. One immediate consequence is that there will be one valedictorian, not eight.

Sixth, and last, I am reorienting the school toward academics and away from politics and propaganda. No more time will be devoted to scaring you about smoking and caffeine, or terrifying you about sexual harassment or global warming. No more semesters will be devoted to condom wearing and teaching you to regard sexual relations as the only or primarily a health issue. There will be no more attempts to convince you that you are a victim because you are not white, or not male, or not heterosexual or not Christian. We will have failed if any one of you graduates this school and does not consider him or herself inordinately lucky—to be alive and to be an American.

Now, please stand and join me in the Pledge of Allegiance to the flag of our country. As many of you do not know the words, our teachers will hand them out to you." —High School principal Dennis Prager of Colorado

My contention is that interpreting the rules is an integral part of the teaching profession.

> *"It should be your care, therefore, and mine, to elevate the minds of our children and exalt their courage; to accelerate and animate their industry and activity; to excite in them a habitual contempt of meanness, abhorrence of injustice and inhumanity, and an ambition to excel in every capacity, faculty, and virtue. If we suffer their minds to grovel and creep in infancy, they will grovel all their lives."* —John Adams, *Dissertation on the Canon and Feudal Law, 1756*

As citizens and parents, we need to understand the difference between the law and the intent of the law. When the intent of the law is perverted the law must be evaluated and rescinded and if need be reissued in a more applicable and productive format. Then we need to demand that public officials and especially those involved in educating our children understand the function and purpose of the rules.

The lawyer's role in these grotesque interpretations of the rules is integral. The language of government, multiculturalism and political correctness has become so convoluted and immersed in legal jargon that every law or regulation is open to endless interpretation by those who are trying to either apply the law, circumvent the law, or enforce the law. In addition, the lawyers have sought to regulate every aspect of the individuals' life. There are now laws to control what we buy, how we speak, how we raise our families, and laws that try to interpret what we think. Lawyers permeate our Senate and House of Representatives. Every year these folks spend nearly every moment not devoted to re election, to conjuring up new and more intrusive laws. They never review the existing laws to rescind those that are duplications, out of date or ineffective.

> *"Laws are made for men of ordinary understanding and*

should, therefore, be construed by the ordinary rules of common sense. Their meaning is not to be sought for in metaphysical subtleties which may make anything mean everything or nothing at pleasure." —Thomas Jefferson, letter to William Johnson, 1823

Recognizing that some form of government is necessary our founders first tried the Articles of Confederation. Having just fought an extended war for independence they were leery of a strong centralized government. The Articles established a government with very little centralized control. The primary power was relegated to the individual states. The Articles failed because they gave too little authority to the Federal government.

"I entirely concur in the propriety of resorting to the sense in which the Constitution was accepted and ratified by the nation. In that sense alone it is the legitimate Constitution. And if that is not the guide in expounding it, there may be no security for a consistent and stable, more than for a faithful exercise of its powers. If the meaning of the text be sought in the changeable meaning of the words composing it, it is evident that the shape and attributes of the Government must partake of the changes to which the words and phrases of all living languages are constantly subject. What a metamorphosis would be produced in the code of law if all its ancient phraseology were to be taken in its modern sense. And that the language of our Constitution is already undergoing interpretations unknown to its founders, will I believe appear to all unbiased Enquirers into the history of its origin and adoption." —James Madison, letter to Henry Lee, 1824

"A constitution founded on these principles introduces knowledge among the people, and inspires them with a conscious dignity becoming freemen; a general emulation takes

place, which causes good humor, sociability, good manners, and good morals to be general. That elevation of sentiment inspired by such a government makes the common people brave and enterprising. That ambition which is inspired by it makes them sober, industrious, and frugal." —John Adams, Thoughts on Government, 1776

For the above to take effect, the people must be educated about the Constitution and its content. The citizens must know and understand their Constitution or freedom is lost.

It is interesting to note that the Bill of Rights were not included in the original draft of the Constitution. At the insistence of Patrick Henry and his fellow states rights and individual rights advocates that the Constitution was ratified with the proviso that the 10 amendments called the Bill of Rights be a guaranteed immediate addition. The role of lawyers in government has, at such times, been very productive and supportive of individual freedom. However, in the ensuing years the lawyers' influence has come to convolute every law or regulation so that it is open to endless interpretation.

"Law and liberty cannot rationally become the objects of our love, unless they first become the objects of our knowledge." —James Wilson, Of the Study of the Law in the United States, 1790

"I should consider the speeches of Livy, Sallust, and Tacitus, as preeminent specimens of logic, taste and that sententious brevity which, using not a word to spare, leaves not a moment for inattention to the hearer. Amplification is the vice of modern oratory." —Thomas Jefferson, letter to David Harding, 1824

Right, Wrong, or Indifferent?

You are losing your freedom, and you are losing the country that was presented to you by the Founding Fathers; a nation that valued the individual. A nation where the citizens were free to achieve all that they could achieve so long as their achievement was not at the expense of another's freedom. I know, slavery was inherent in the culture at the founding. However, careful reading of the thoughts and notes left by the founders makes it clear that though they accepted the presence of slavery in their culture at their time it was considered an evil to be addressed in time. They looked forward to the fulfillment of the promise in the words of the Declaration of Independence and the Constitution. Now you are being coerced by politicians and history revisionists to accept the unacceptable. Though the freedom illustrated in the founding documents has evolved over the ensuing years, it did not require that the Constitution be abandoned; it required that the intent of those documents be fulfilled.

The Family

Do you believe that the family unit is the foundation of all civil societies? The family unit we know is a mother, a father, and children living together as a cohesive unit. That unit is the foundation of successful cultures. This includes the extended family of grandparents, aunts, uncles and cousins. Now the state is telling you that this is not really true. A father, or in some cases, a mother, is not necessary to complete a family.

> *"The foundation of national morality must be laid in private families. ... How is it possible that Children can have any just Sense of the sacred Obligations of Morality or Religion if, from their earliest Infancy, they learn their Mothers live in habitual Infidelity to their fathers, and their fathers in as constant Infidelity to their Mothers?"* —John Adams, Diary, 1778

The state can and will take the place of either parental figure and provide for the single parent and the children. The father, because of the organization of the welfare state, is encouraged to be absent from the family structure. He is not held responsible for the health and well-being of the children he fathers. He can impregnate and move on. The state will attend to his offspring, more or less, and for the mother, in a minimal manner. Do you believe that a mother is a woman, the father, a man; that the father and mother as the parents; are responsible for the care and nurturing of their children? Is it true that parents are to prepare their children to be productive members of the community? Do you believe that parents understand and accept this responsibility as their own? If you said yes, you are mistaken. We are being indoctrinated to believe that it is the state's responsibility to assure that the children are cared for, nurtured, educated, and placed into society as a productive member of the state- more or less. Now you are told that the family unit is nothing special. You are to accept that a family without a father, or in some cases without a mother, is just as normal as the traditional family. You are forced to accept that a family is any one or two persons who decide to call themselves a family. Two men can choose to be a marriage; two women can choose to be a marriage. Though you believe in your heart of hearts that this isn't really a marriage, we are now forced, by the state, to accept homosexual and lesbian relationships as equal to heterosexual relationships, as a marriage. Now marriage has been redefined to mean whatever we want it to mean. We are told that marriage is nothing special, even though we believe in our hearts that it is. A relationship composed of two men or two women, we are told is a marriage, just as normal and natural as the marriage we recognize as a unique relationship instituted to stabilize societies and to produce children. The same sex relationship cannot produce children, but, should they decide that they would like to have children to add to the relationship, by whatever means, we are told that we must accept this as equal to the traditional family. We are routinely admonished to be open minded and accepting of all situations we might encounter. We are grilled that we should never offend anyone just because they don't comply with what we believe is right or normal. No matter how much we may be offended by being forced to embrace these aberrations of our beliefs, we are to bear it all with kind consideration for the offenders. We, should we make the mistake of making it obvious that the aberrant activities offend us, are not allowed the same kind consideration. We are publicly ridiculed, dragged into court for hate crimes, and in danger of fines and imprisonment for making our beliefs known.

At the beginning of the school year, gay pride events at a military academy with titles like "condom Olympics" and "queer prom" would have been unthinkable. This week, they're a reality. http://times247.com/articles/gay-pride-week-comes-to-oldest-u-s-military-school#ixzz1qMWvNYvn

So, essentially, what our nation of free people is affirming is that those who base their lives on their belief in a Divine Creator, are unique in the population. These believers are the only individuals who the rest of the population are free to offend without any fear of condemnation, retribution or reprisal.

I have no desire to persecute homosexuals or lesbians. I do believe in the Golden Rule. My faith tells me that homosexual practice is not right or normal. I do not believe that those who are so inclined choose that particular lifestyle. Therefore, I believe that they should be treated with all the respect and deference afforded every other human being. I do not believe that either homosexuality or lesbianism should be glorified or condemned. It is neither good nor bad. It is an aberration of the natural order of things. Some may say that these have always existed and therefore are normal and natural. Please, birth defects have always existed also, but we don't consider them normal or the natural order. It is what it is, so accept it for what it is and proceed to make life a pleasure for everyone. If they want to call each other husband and wife, fine. I have no problem with them establishing a household built on mutual love and respect. I do not believe that they should be denied any of the rights and privileges of every other citizen. However, don't demand that I put aside what I believe to be right and replace my faith with situational ethics. I have pretty simple beliefs. If a homosexual is talented as an artist or musician or mathematician or whatever, they should be admired for their talent. I don't believe that their sexual orientation is the source of their talent or their ability. Homosexuality is neither to be glorified nor ridiculed. To complicate matters we now have a generation of parents who have decided that their pre-teen children must be introduced to gender choice. This is to make them sensitive to those who have difficulty with the gender nature assigned them. The teen years are difficult enough without adding the requirement that one must embrace and try out the characteristics of their sexual opposites. If you disagree with me, fine. Don't get a sign and march around my house condemning me for what I believe. Give me and my beliefs the same consideration you demand that I give to you and yours. We can agree to disagree and move on to enjoy life. Our sexual preferences are no ones' business but our own and our chosen partner. It is not a government concern.

There are many situations, now celebrated, that a couple of generations ago were considered in poor taste, the result of poor choice, not a subject to be discussed in the presence of children. That was a few of generations ago. Today…we seem to be engaged in compulsory appreciation of any and all social aberrations.

Premarital sex, illegitimate births, co-habitation, profane language, abortion, divorce, these are all symptoms of a cultural breakdown.

So, there you have it. One citizen's appraisal of the status of the rules, regulations and laws instituted by government's leadership. A perspective on the status of our culture and where it is drifting to. It's time to change course before the ship of state runs aground.

How Can We Change Course?

- A good starting point would be to re-introduce God into the public sphere. Reemphasize the whole of the first amendment. Especially the part that states "or prohibiting the free exercise thereof:". Acknowledge that faith in a Creator was instrumental in the life and values of the Founding Fathers. The Judeo-Christian fundamentals are the foundation of our cultural values. If you are a non believer that's fine; but consider this: What harm is there in teaching and accepting the tenets of Exodus Chapter 20 and Matthew Chapter 5. How bad can a world be where we do not covet what isn't ours; where to lie, steal, and murder is universally condemned? How bad would it be to treat your neighbor as you would prefer to be treated? Why is it ridiculed to believe in an Intelligent Creator? It would be a positive move to put God back into the public arena and emphasize the values in the Gospel message as the core values for our culture.

- Mandatory education regarding the content and the intent of the Constitution is necessary. K thru 12 and all college degrees should require definitive knowledge of the history and content of the Constitution.

- Removing the necessity for extreme wealth to be a viable candidate for political office. Limit the amount of money that can be invested in pursuit of elective office.

- Institute term limits on all elected or appointed federal positions, including Executive, Judicial, and Legislative.

- Appointment to positions in the federal bureaucracy must be a strict meritocracy bound by adherence to the Constitution and promotion attained by productivity without regard to tenure.

- Limit campaigning for office to 12 months prior to the election.

- Limit political donations to individual donations only and a maximum amount no greater than a percentage of the average annual individual income of the nation. The expense involved in running for political office is ridiculous. Only the extremely wealthy can afford to run, or someone who is backed by a shadow group of supporters who do not want their agenda to be exposed.

- Remove all lobbyists from Washington D.C. No lobbyist offices can be located within 150 miles of the capitol. The truth is- those lobbying organizations are poorly disguised consummately determined bribery machines. It is good that we can "lobby" our representatives. However, when the lobbying by corporations and financial institutions includes large sums of money, or in-kind gifts, in exchange for support of laws that result in financial benefits for a particular organization or person, it is bribery.

- All politicians should be denied lobbyist credentials with any company or corporation doing business with the federal government for a minimum of 10 years after leaving political office.

- Institute a flat tax. The IRS is an organization that has too much power. It operates outside the rights we are guaranteed in our Bill of Rights.

- Remove enforcement power from all departments such as the IRS, EPA, FAA, FCC, etc. If they find violations that they want addressed, these departments should have to use normal channels of law enforcement and the judicial system. They should require "just cause" warrants issued by judicial authority and served through normal law enforcement channels. There should be no law enforcement power delegated to bureaucratic offices of the state or federal government.

- The House and Senate should be prohibited from adding amendments to proposed bills that have nothing to do with the intent of the bill. Adding, to a bill that is sure to pass, an amendment that institutes a law that could not be passed on its own merit is a deceptive tactic practiced by both parties. Each bill proposed should be a clean bill confined to the purpose and intent of that bill only. In addition, every law passed should have a mandatory sunset clause. A date where the law must be reviewed and it should either be renewed with a new sunset date or it should expire.

We have now elected a non-politician to lead the nation as chief executive. This is the result of the growing contempt for the career politicians who have put the nation and our freedom in dire straits. It may, or may not, have positive results. But until we address the cause for the national discontent, we will see an ongoing effort by the voters to correct the situation via the ballot box.

Thanks for the opportunity to vent. I will close with this admonition. If we don't take corrective action soon, the time is inevitable when the correction will be initiated by violence. I fear for my grandchildren and great grandchildren should that ever happen.

"I know the American People are much attached to their Government;—I know they would suffer much for its sake;—

I know they would endure evils long and patiently, before they would ever think of exchanging it for another. Yet, notwithstanding all this, if the laws be continually despised and disregarded, if their rights to be secure in their persons and property, are held by no better tenure than the caprice of a mob, the alienation of their affections from the Government is the natural consequence; and to that, sooner or later, it must come." —*Abraham Lincoln's Lyceum Speech—1838*

There is a great tragedy and great suffering involved in revolution. We can spare ourselves if we will act while rationality has a chance. Just sayin'—Shalom

Endnotes

1. Supreme Court Hears Colorado Bakery Case Highlighting Clash Between US Laws, voanews.com, December 05, 2017
2. Montebello high school in Montebello, California, Monday, March 27, 2006
3. Office for Civil Rights (2006). Questions and Answers on the Rights of Limited-English Proficient Students
4. In 1970, the federal Office for Civil Rights (OCR) issued a memo regarding school districts' responsibilities under civil rights law to provide an equal educational opportunity to ELLs. This memorandum stated:
   Where the inability to speak and understand the English language excludes national origin minority group children from effective participation in the educational program offered by a school district, the district must take affirmative steps to rectify the language deficiency in order to open its instructional program to these students.
5. Newsweek U.S. Edition Fri, Sep 29, 2017 Immigrants Are Getting the Right to Vote in Cities Across America by John Haltiwanger On 9/13/17 at 3:57 PM
6. "Parents' Religion and Children's Welfare: Debunking the Doctrine of Parents' Rights,"